THE LIVING WORLD

HOW PLANTS GROW

Malcolm Penny

W
FRANKLIN WATTS
LONDON • SYDNEY

This edition first published in 2003 by
Franklin Watts
96 Leonard Street
London
EC2A 4XD

Franklin Watts Australia
45-51 Huntley Street
Alexandria
NSW 2015

ISBN: 0 7496 5146 6

A CIP catalogue reference for this book is available
from the British Library.

© Marshall Cavendish Corporation, 1997, 2003

Series created by Discovery Books Ltd.
Originally published as *Nature's Mysteries: How Plants Grow*
by Marshall Cavendish Corporation,
99 White Plains Road, Tarrytown, NY, 10591, USA.

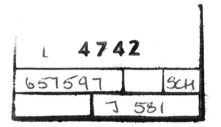

Printed in Malaysia

Acknowledgments
Illustrated by Stuart Lafford
The publishers would like to thank the following for their permission to reproduce photographs: cover Eric
Crichton/Bruce Coleman, title page Alex Ramsay, 5 top Steven C. Kaufman/Bruce Coleman, 5 bottom Dr. Eckart
Pott/Bruce Coleman, 6-7 G.A. Maclean/Oxford Scientific Films, 7 Eric Crichton/Bruce Coleman, 9 top Kim Taylor/Bruce
Coleman, 9 bottom Christian Zuber/Bruce Coleman, 13 top Dr. Jeremy Burgess/Science Photo Library, 13 bottom John
Shaw/Bruce Coleman, 14 Gerald Cubitt/Bruce Coleman, 14-15 John Shaw/Bruce Coleman, 15 Johnny Johnson/Bruce
Coleman, 17 John Shaw/Bruce Coleman, 18 left George McCarthy/Bruce Coleman, 18 right Adrian Davies/Bruce
Coleman, 19 top Marie Read/Bruce Coleman, 19 bottom Jan Taylor/Bruce Coleman, 21 top Kim Taylor/Bruce Coleman,
21 bottom Jane Burton/Bruce Coleman, 22 left Tim Shepherd/Oxford Scientific Films, 22 right Alain Compost/Bruce
Coleman, 23 top Barbara C. Harrison/Oxford Scientific Films, 23 bottom John & Irene Palmer/Survival Anglia/Oxford
Scientific Films, 24 left Jeff Foott Productions/Bruce Coleman, 24 right Philip Sharpe/Oxford Scientific Films, 25 M.P.L.
Fogden/Bruce Coleman, 27 top David Tipling/Oxford Scientific Films, 27 bottom Ronald Toms/Oxford Scientific Films,
29 left Alex Ramsay, 29 right Erwin & Peggy Bauer/Bruce Coleman

(Cover) A passion flower fully open attracts pollinators.

CONTENTS

THE WORLD OF PLANTS

Over millions of years, plants have conquered the world. They can grow almost everywhere, even in places where animals can survive for only a short time. Among the few places where plants can't live are the polar ice caps, the tops of the highest mountains, and the bottom of the deepest seas.

This food chain shows how animals in the cold Arctic finally depend on plants, even if their main food is other animals. A polar bear eats seals, seals eat fish, fish eat smaller fish, and small fish eat shrimp. So far, these are all animals eating animals. But shrimp eat tiny plants that float in the sea. So, even the polar bear depends on plants.

All life on Earth depends on plants. Even animals that eat only other animals need plants for their prey to feed on. A list of what eats what is called a food chain. Plants are the basis of all food chains. In the end, even large meat-eating animals depend on plants.

All plants grow in the same way and almost all make their own food. To do this, they need just a few simple things: water, carbon dioxide, sunlight, and salts from the ground. Plants also produce something extra that is essential for most forms of life — oxygen, which all animals breathe.

▲ *The highest mountains are too cold for plants. Here, you can see the treeline, the place beyond which plants cannot grow.*

To flourish, plants must push roots down and stems up. And when a plant is damaged — by people, other animals, or weather — it must repair itself. We'll see how all these tasks are accomplished.

Most plants follow a growth cycle of flowering, pollination, seeding, germination, and development of flowers again. Perennial plants and trees can repeat this cycle over and over again for many years. Annual plants produce seeds only once and then die.

Cactus plants can grow in very barren places, if they can find just a little fresh water to store in their stems. These are growing on lava in the Galapagos Islands.

THE GLORY OF FLOWERS

The most colourful and noticeable parts of many plants are their flowers. Flowers come in many different shapes and sizes, but they all follow the same basic plan. They are formed at different times of the year. Mostly this is in spring or summer, but some plants flower in autumn and a few flower in the winter. At the right time for the flower to form, some of the plant's growing tips begin to develop in a completely different way. Instead of growing upward, the tips become swollen and produce four rings of special leaves.

The first ring is made of the sepals. They are green and mostly like ordinary leaves. They protect the rings developing inside them. The next ring is composed of the flower petals, thin and often very colourful. Within the petals is a ring of stamens with anthers at their tips. Anthers produce pollen, the male sex cells. Inside the stamens is an ovary containing unfertilized female eggs, joined by a stalk called a style to a sticky stigma on top.

Flowers exist to make seeds. But to do so, they must first be pollinated. Many plants are pollinated by insects attracted by the flower's scent or bright patterns. At the base of the petals, nectaries produce sweet nectar that many insects use for food. Insects collect and eat the pollen, too.

Pollination happens when an insect that has been scrambling around one flower, collecting nectar and pollen,

In a typical flower, the male and female parts are in the centre, surrounded by colourful petals that attract pollinators and by sepals that protect the flower as it forms.

Petal

Stigma

Style

Anther

Stamen

Sepal

Ovary

flies off to feed at another. It will have pollen grains clinging to its body, and as it crawls into the next flower, some of these grains stick to the stigma. Soon, one or more of them grows down into the ovary to fertilize the waiting eggs. A fertilized egg grows into a seed. Next, the seed must get to a good place to grow.

▼ *A honeybee feeding on an apple blossom. As the bee sucks out the nectar, its body becomes covered in pollen grains, which it brushes off with its legs, collecting them in bristly pollen baskets on its back legs. The yellow clump of pollen is easy to see. The bee will visit other flowers, and some of the pollen will be brushed onto them.*

▲ *Small insects perching on the long stigma of a passion flower will leave pollen grains from other flowers they have visited.*

JUICY FRUITS AND PARACHUTES

If a parent plant just dropped all its seeds around itself, the patch of ground on which it stood would soon become very overcrowded. Plants therefore try to spread their seeds as widely as possible and they do this by many different methods. Some produce sweet, fleshy fruits, like apples or raspberries, that animals like to eat. When the animals move away, the seeds pass through their stomach and intestines unharmed and fall to

Other seeds are wrapped in thorny fruits, like burrs, covered with spines or hooks. They, too, are transported by animals but on their outside, hooked onto the animals' fur or stuck into their skin. Eventually, an animal will groom itself, and the seeds will drop off far from where they started.

A third way of spreading seeds is on the wind. Sycamore trees produce seeds with wings that spin as they fall,

---

Packages of New Life: Some of the Wide Variety of Plant Fruits.

◄ *The seed capsule of the grapple plant has sharp hooks that point in several directions. This allows it to be caught up and carried away on the soles of elephants and rhinos.*

► *The sycamore seed has wings attached to it to help it travel some distance from the tree that produced it.*

► *Fig trees produce sweet fruit that many animals like to eat. These animals then spread the seeds widely in their droppings.*

► *The birdcage plant dies and curls up into a ball, which is blown by wind across the desert. When it reaches a sheltered place, heat splits the seed pods, and the seeds fall out.*

---

the ground in the animals' droppings. With luck, some of these seeds will then be in a suitable place to grow, surrounded by fertilizer.

drifting away downwind to land away from their parent tree. Thistles and dandelions grow a silky tuft on each seed, like a tiny parachute. The wind

▼ *Coconuts can drift thousands of miles across the sea and germinate anywhere above the high-tide line. This one may have started growing too close to the water.*

▲ *Thistledown floats miles on the breeze, but these seeds won't reach the ground unless the spider's web is knocked down or falls.*

may carry their seeds for miles before dropping them gently to the ground.

Some trees have their seeds planted for them by animals. Nuts and acorns are spread through the forest by squirrels that store food for the winter by burying them in the ground. Although the squirrels come back and dig most of them up, the ones they forget grow into new trees.

SHOOTS UP, ROOTS DOWN

Some seeds may spend months or even years waiting for the right moment to germinate, or sprout growing tips. Others germinate very quickly. Growing tips reach up if they are shoots and down if they are roots.

A new plant is born! When a seed lands in a suitable place with warmth and water, its coat splits and the root breaks out and grows down through the soil. The first shoot moves up toward the light. Then it quickly produces leaves, while the root burrows deeper into the ground.

◀ *When light comes from only one side, plants grow toward it. If you grow plants indoors by a window, you might want to turn the pot around from time to time to make them grow straight.*

Shoots grow toward light. If the light is coming from just one side of a growing shoot, the shoot will grow quicker on the opposite side, bending the shoot toward the light.

Roots do not respond to light but both shoots and roots respond to the Earth's pull — gravity. If a shoot and root are laid flat on the ground, gravity will cause changes within the plant, making the shoots grow upward and the roots downward.

Plants suck up water and chemicals in the ground through their roots, which are really just tubes pushed into the soil with smaller tubes growing out of them. These smaller tubes in turn are covered with still tinier tubes called root hairs. The wall of the root hair will only allow water and certain chemicals to pass through it.

A plant sucks up water without using any energy. The water moves up the roots into the stem and leaves of the plant, ready to be used to make food. But the plant also needs some of the chemicals from the soil to grow properly. It must use energy to draw them into its root hairs. The energy has to come from the food the plant has already made. But how *does* the plant make food?

Water and chemicals from the soil pass through the very thin walls of tiny hairs on a plant's roots. From there, they travel up through tubes to the leaves. When water evaporates from the leaves, more is drawn up from the ground to replace it.

ENERGY AND GROWTH

Green plants make food by combining water from the soil and a gas called carbon dioxide from the air in a process called photosynthesis. Photosynthesis needs sunlight to provide the energy to make it happen. A chemical in the plant, a pigment called chlorophyll, traps the energy from the sun and releases it so that a chemical change can take place.

When the water and carbon dioxide are combined, they produce a sugar called glucose. The oxygen from the water is not needed so it is passed out of the plant as a waste product. Meanwhile, the glucose stores energy from the sun. The plant uses this energy to collect salts from the soil and to grow. Some glucose is changed into starch, which the plant can store to use later.

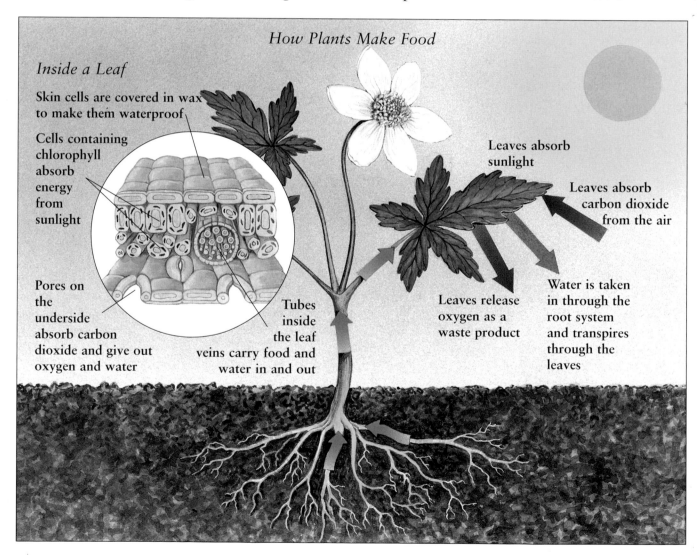

How Plants Make Food

Inside a Leaf

Skin cells are covered in wax to make them waterproof

Cells containing chlorophyll absorb energy from sunlight

Pores on the underside absorb carbon dioxide and give out oxygen and water

Tubes inside the leaf veins carry food and water in and out

Leaves absorb sunlight

Leaves absorb carbon dioxide from the air

Leaves release oxygen as a waste product

Water is taken in through the root system and transpires through the leaves

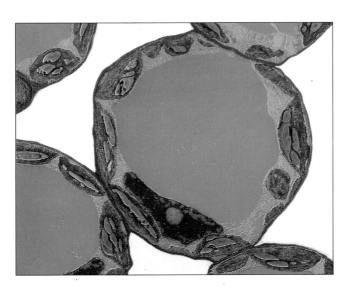

▲ *A plant cell magnified thousands of times larger than life. The nucleus of the cell has been coloured red, and the parts that contain the chlorophyll are green. The pink areas inside are starch, the stored sugar the plant needs for energy.*

All living creatures are made up of cells. Plant cells are like little boxes with walls made of cellulose. Inside the cell is the chlorophyll that the plant uses to provide energy. Also inside the cell is the nucleus, which controls everything the cell does.

Cells are the building blocks of a plant. For a plant to grow, its cells must divide to make more building blocks. The nucleus divides first, then the rest of the cell divides into two, and a new wall grows across the middle. When the new cells have grown big enough, they, too, will divide. In a growing root or a shoot, cells divide only at the very tip. The part behind the tip contains young cells that can expand quickly to extend the root or shoot in the right direction.

▼ *In autumn, trees withdraw chlorophyll from their leaves, leaving only waste products in the otherwise empty cells. This is what produces the glorious red and orange colours of trees like maples.*

WRAPPING AND REPAIRS

All roots, and some special types of shoot, respond to touch. If a root meets a stone, it turns away from it until the soil is clear for it to burrow farther down. Some climbing plants wrap themselves around anything they touch. Bindweed, string beans, and strangler figs all climb in this way.

▼ *A strangler fig around a mopane tree in Namibia. It grew down from the branch where its seed germinated. When the dead tree has rotted away, the fig may be able to stand without support.*

Most plants grow from the tip of the shoot, but grasses are different. The tops of their leaves are eaten by many kinds of animals or chopped off by lawn mowers so they need to grow from the bottom of the leaf, which is undamaged.

▶ *Wildebeest cropping grass in East Africa. Grasses survive this attack by growing again from the bottom of the leaf, rather than from the top of the shoot.*

14

When winter is over and as the nights shorten, plants begin to grow. This Texas prairie in spring is a mass of competing advertisements to pollinators.

Animals eat bushy plants as well, usually biting off the tender growing tips. The plants respond by abandoning that growing point and starting new ones on side shoots, making the plant even bushier. Clipping a hedge makes it grow more thickly for this reason.

Plants can tell the time of year by the changing length of the night. A special blue pigment in the leaves reacts differently to light and darkness. As the nights get shorter, a new sequence of events in the plant is set off, preparing it for spring.

FRIENDS IN THE FOREST

Pine forests like those in the United States Pacific Northwest have a special way of growing, involving several kinds of fungi that grow in the ground, deer mice, and flying squirrels. The fungus grows underground as fine filaments, like hairs, wrapped round the smallest roots of the trees. The filaments absorb salts from the ground and pass them to the roots, supplying the tree with the chemicals it needs to grow. This saves the tree energy since it does

An ancient forest is a web in which the animals and plants help each other. This web may take a hundred years to develop fully. Newly planted forests lack most of the elements of the web.

not have to absorb the salts for itself. In return, the fungus takes a little sugar from the tree to help it to grow. A relationship like this, where both plants help each other, is called symbiosis, which means "living together."

Dead trees, standing or fallen, are an important part of the ancient forest, providing nesting places for birds and nutrients for the plants around them.

Most fungi produce their fruits above ground as mushrooms or toadstools, but the pine forest fungi produce underground fruits called truffles. The truffles have a very strong smell, which mice and squirrels (and a lot of people) find delicious. The animals sniff them out and dig them up to eat. (People use specially trained pigs to find this delicacy.) When the animals have digested the truffles, the tiny seeds of the fungus, called spores, are scattered in the animal's droppings. So the animals are well fed, the fungus is spread further through the forest, and the trees grow better than they could have done on their own.

17

PLANTS THAT STEAL FOOD

Pine root fungi cannot make their own food. Instead, they take what they need from the trees in exchange for the salts that they give the trees. Other fungi give nothing back but simply steal their food from other living plants. They are called parasites.

Not all fungi are parasites. Some, like bracket fungi, get their food from the rotting remains of dead plants.

Growing as a mass of filaments inside dead tree trunks, they are invisible for most of the year until they produce fruiting bodies in the autumn. The fruiting bodies stick out of the tree and produce spores that spread the fungus to other dead trees.

▼ Dodder is a parasite that has no leaves. It invades the stems of different plants and sucks out water and nutrients until the host plant dies.

▲ Bracket fungi often appear on trunks of dead trees. They have a waterproof upper surface and gills underneath, where the spores are produced in the autumn.

rhododendrons. The leaves of the Indian pipe are useless - tiny, colourless scales with no chlorophyll.

Some green parasites use chlorophyll to make food but steal the water they need. The mistletoe family contains over a thousand different species. Instead of putting down roots into the ground, mistletoe pushes them into the trunk or branch of a tree and sucks out the sap.

▼ *The Australian Christmas tree grows up to fourteen metres tall. Its roots reach out to those of other nearby plants and steal water from them.*

▲ *The ghostly stems and flowers of the parasitic Indian pipe stand about fifteen centimetres high on a shady pine forest floor.*

A parasitic plant called Indian pipe also grows in pine forests. Its roots weave among the fungi, sucking out the sugar that they obtained from the trees. It gives nothing back, either to the trees or to the fungi. Although Indian pipe is a parasite, it is not a fungus but a green plant. Its closest relations are heathers and

INSECT-EATING PLANTS

Some plants that live in poor soil have to get their food by eating animals, mainly insects. These plants are called carnivorous plants.

Pitcher plants have tube-shaped leaves, filled with liquid. At the open end are glands producing sweet-smelling

A deadly trap: Pitcher plants cannot get enough food from the ground, so they attract insects to eat.

nectar. Insects attracted by the scent climb into the tube to feed. But the inside is slippery, and they fall into the liquid and drown. As their bodies decay, the plant absorbs the nutrients that it cannot obtain from the ground. Some pitcher plants produce a liquid that actually digests their victims.

Sundews' leaves are covered with hairs, each with a tiny bead of glue on the end. An insect landing on the leaf sticks to any hair it touches. As it struggles, other hairs bend toward it by growing very quickly on the side away from the insect. They can bend right over in less than a minute. If the insect is large, the whole leaf may curl around it. The glue is also a digestive fluid, dissolving the insect until the hairs can absorb it.

The Venus flytrap has two lobes at the end of each leaf, hinged in the middle and edged with a row of spikes. Below the spikes are nectar glands, and each lobe bears a few trigger hairs. Insects attracted by the nectar crawl over the open lobes. If they touch one of the hairs just once, nothing happens, but if they touch it again within twenty seconds the trap closes in less than one third of a second. A small insect can still crawl

▲ *One touch is enough for this lacewing to be trapped by the sundew's tubular glue-tipped hairs. They will gradually digest it and absorb the resulting liquid.*

out from between the spikes, but larger insects trying to escape touch the trigger hairs a third time. When this happens, cells in the lobes begin to grow rapidly, so that the trap shuts tightly. Then the poor insect is soaked in digestive acid and dissolved.

The Venus flytrap lives naturally only in marshes on the border between North and South Carolina, but all over the world, people keep them as plant "pets."

UNUSUAL PLANTS

The world is filled with many other weird and wonderful plants, which have developed unusual ways to grow or get themselves noticed by pollinators. Many orchids look and smell like certain female bees and wasps. Males of those species visit the flower thinking they have found a mate, and pollinate the orchid at the same time.

▲ *The fly orchid's flowers imitate insects, attracting flies that try to mate with them and pollinate them in the process.*

The Brazilian birthwort flower looks like meat and smells like rotting fish. Though humans find it very unpleasant, the flower is very attractive to the flies that pollinate it.

Perhaps the most unusual flower of all, however, is one that grows in the forests of Borneo and Sumatra. There lives a mysterious parasitic plant called the rafflesia. The only part of it that is visible without the aid of a microscope is the flower. But that can grow to be enormous, often over ninety centimetres across!

▼ *A rafflesia flower in Sumatra. It grows as a parasite on the roots of forest vines and flowers only for three or four days each year. Then it rots to a pile of black slime.*

▲ *A gnarled veteran of history: a bristlecone pine in Great Basin National Park, Nevada. Most of the twisted trunk is dead, with just a string of living tissue in the middle.*

Some plants go to extremes, of size, or age, way beyond what others can do. A bristlecone pine tree growing on Wheeler Peak, Nevada, is 4,900 years old, which makes it the oldest living thing on Earth. The biggest living thing on Earth is a coast redwood, a type of sequoia tree in Humboldt Redwoods State Park, California, which stands 110 metres tall.

▶ *Giant sequoias from California are the largest trees in the world. The biggest of them are more than 3000 years old and weigh more than 1,800 tonnes.*

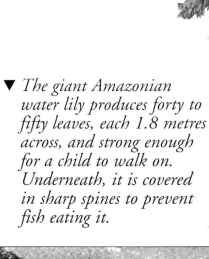

▼ *The giant Amazonian water lily produces forty to fifty leaves, each 1.8 metres across, and strong enough for a child to walk on. Underneath, it is covered in sharp spines to prevent fish eating it.*

PLANT ADAPTATIONS

Hot, bright climates or cool, dim conditions are not ideal for growing plants. Many plants have had to adapt to survive and grow in less-than-perfect situations.

grow only in North and South America, have no leaves at all. They carry out photosynthesis in their stems, which they can also fill with water to use when they need it.

Instead of leaves, they have spines that protect them from thirsty animals trying to eat them.

Holly and thistles also use spines to protect their leaves from being eaten, while some plants, among them certain oak trees, produce chemicals that taste bad to the insects that try to eat their leaves.

▲ *Giant barrel cacti in Baja California, with an elephant tree in the foreground. Only specialized plants can survive and grow in this parched ground.*

In deserts where it is very hot and dry, plants have to protect themselves against losing too much water through the pores in their leaves. Some do it by having very few pores and some by having leaves covered in a waxy, waterproof layer. Cacti, which

Acacia trees in Costa Rica provide nectar for ants to eat; in return, the ants keep away animals that try to eat the tree.

Another problem for plants is too little light. The floor of a forest may be very shady because the trees above have blocked out the light before it can reach the ground. Some plants overcome this by having very large leaves to make the best use of whatever light reaches them. Others have a layer of red cells on the lower surface of their leaves to reflect the light back to pass through the leaf a second time.

Deep in the shade of the rain forest, ferns and some types of palm can grow in the darkness because they have extremely large leaves that collect all the available light. The red flowers are those of heliconia, sometimes called lobster claw.

The most specialized leaves are those of begonia plants that grow in Asian forests. They have tiny lenses in the upper surface of their leaves to focus light onto their energy-producing cells.

WAR ON PLANTS

Ever since people began growing plants for food — and for enjoyment in gardens — they have regarded certain plants as weeds. A weed is basically a plant growing in the wrong place. It might be a dandelion spoiling a lawn, grass in a flower bed, or poppies growing among corn stalks. As scientists learned more about how plants grow, they invented ways of destroying them with weed killers.

Some chemicals kill all of the plants they touch, working in one of two ways. Systemic weed killers work by interfering with photosynthesis, preventing the plant from making new food. They also stop the release of food stores from roots or stems. Hormonal weed killers make the plant grow so fast that it uses up its energy reserves faster than it can replace them.

Other weed killers are selective, killing only certain kinds of plants. Some kill grass, leaving plants with broad leaves unharmed, while other weed killers work the other way.

On farms, weed killers are usually applied by spraying. The dangers are easy to see. On a windy day, chemicals might be blown to where

Selective Weed Killer in a Garden

A lawn full of broad-leaved weeds is sprayed with a selective weed killer.

Soon, the broad-leaved plants wilt and die, while the grass remains unharmed.

Wild poppies only grow along the edges of fields of crops where weed killers haven't reached.

into the water table underground. From there, weed killers can enter drinking water through wells. Studies of plants have revealed ways of harming only those that we regard as weeds, but the chemicals involved are powerful and need to be used with great care and precision.

they're not wanted. Some are harmful to humans or animals, while others can cause damage when they are washed into streams or ponds or sink

▼ *The chemicals that farmers spray over their fields to control weeds can affect people's gardens, and the people themselves, if they are not used with great care. Rivers and ponds may also be harmed.*

A WORLD SUITABLE FOR PLANTS

Plants need the right conditions to grow. First, the soil must contain the right amount of water. Some plants like dry conditions and others wet ground. The ground must also be free from harmful chemicals that can soak into the water table and damage plants when they draw the poisoned water up into their roots. Third, plants need clean air. Smoke fumes from a factory can kill plants as effectively as any weed killer.

Building dams that flood forests and prairies or draining swamps and marshes are two other ways of damaging the plant life of the world. Acid rain is another. All rain contains some weak and harmless acids because it dissolves natural carbon

We pollute the air with gases from power stations, factories, cars, and homes when we burn fuel. These gases rise into the air and mix with water to fall as acid rain, killing trees all over Europe and North America.

dioxide and sulphur dioxide in the air, but acid rain is produced when fossil fuels are burned, releasing sulphur and nitrogen. These chemicals react with damp air to produce strong sulphuric and nitric acids, which may fall far away from the place where they were produced. Acid rain kills trees, including the famous maple forests of North America.

Forests, marshes, and grasslands — all areas teeming with plants — are very important to humans and to all other life on Earth. Plants take up more carbon dioxide than they produce, keeping it out of the atmosphere and reducing global warming. They also produce more oxygen than they use for every other life form to breathe. Many plants are useful as medicines or food, including wild plants in distant places that scientists have not yet explored. For our health and the health of our planet, we must protect and foster the world's plants.

The rosy periwinkle grows in the forests of Madagascar. Its leaves contain a substance that can cure certain forms of cancer.

◀ *The glory of a well-tended flower garden. Beautiful plants give us great pleasure, but they do much more than that: For food, fuel, and medicines, as well as the oxygen we breathe, we simply could not survive without them.*

GLOSSARY

cellulose: the thin stiff material that forms the walls of plant cells.

fertilizer: a mixture that helps plants to grow. Some fertilizers are natural, like animal droppings, and others may be artificial.

filament: a very thin tube.

global warming: the process by which Earth is getting warmer because of changes in the atmosphere caused by human actions.

hormonal: using hormones, chemicals that change the actions of plants or animals.

nutrients: substances that plants and animals need in order to grow.

pigment: a coloured substance.

pore: a very small hole.

water table: the natural level of water in the soil. In dry places, it may be down very deep.

USEFUL WEBSITES

To find out more about how plants grow, visit some of the websites listed below. You can also use them to explore other aspects of the living world, and to get involved in nature events across the UK and Australia.

Visit **www.urbanext.uiuc.edu/gpe** to experience the 'The Great Plant Escape'! In this fun and up-to-date interactive site children help characters like 'Leplant' and 'Sprout' to solve a range of 'Great Plant Mysteries'!

For more information about individual plants visit **www.yahooligans.com** and click on the **Science and Nature** category. The site includes great photographs and fascinating facts about many different types of plants.

The 'Cool Science for Curious Kids' website at **www.hhmi.org/coolscience** is another great interactive site covering a wide range of science topics.

The Young People's Trust for the Environment is a charity which helps children and young adults explore and understand the environment. The website at **www.yptenc.org.uk** gives up-to-date reports on environmental issues. You will also find lots of ideas on how to get involved in environmental work and events.

Channel 4's excellent educational website provides students and teachers with all the essentials. For help with tricky topics like microorganisms or how things move, visit **www.channel4.com/weblogic/essentials/science/life/index.jsp**

The children's BBC wildlife website at **www.bbc.co.uk/cbbc/wild** is a fun and informative site, with easy links to other educational wildlife sites.

To explore Australia's vast and varied natural environment visit **www.ea.gov.au/education/activities**. This site includes great quizzes, games and activities for children as well as teaching support materials for teachers.

Note to parents and teachers
Every effort has been made by the Publishers to ensure that these websites are suitable for children; that they are of the highest educational value, and that they contain no inappropriate or offensive material.
However, because of the nature of the Internet, it is impossible to guarantee that the contents of these sites will not be altered. We strongly advise that Internet access is supervised by a responsible adult.

INDEX

Numbers in *italic* indicate pictures